the NEXT LEVEL

WWJD

4 complete youth meetings on discipleship that guide students through the NEXT Level Spiritual Challenge Journal

ZondervanPublishingHouse
Grand Rapids, Michigan
A Division of HarperCollins*Publishers*

NEXT Level Leader's Guide

Youth Specialties Books, 300 S. Pierce St., El Cajon, CA 92021, are published by Zondervan Publishing House, 5300 Patterson Ave. S.E., Grand Rapids, MI 49530.

Written by Randy Southern
Edited by Cheri McLaughlin
Cover and interior design by Patton Brothers Design

Printed in the United States of America

ISBN 0-310-22986-3

99 00 01 02 03/ /10 9 8 7 6 5 4 3 2

Contents

Quick guide to song lyrics handouts

Level. Asking "What would Jesus do?" is a place to start

holding distills into four sessions the discipleship insights
dings in their *NEXT Level Spiritual Challenge Journals*. At
culum is a "prep talk" of sorts intended for *you*. Then read
nall-group teachers to read through) the session completely,
nd options of the session that you want to hit. There's
d in a session, so pick and choose what you and your youth

ities (or calm versions of wild activities)... a few options
to prepare for, but that add an unforgettable touch to the
e intriguing and others less complicated...Bible studies
and extensions for those who want them) designed to fit just about any youth group. Of course, you best know the needs and sensitivities of your youth group, so use your freedom to tweak and adapt and drop and add as much as you want.

(Want to tap a huge source of discussion material? If your kids are using the companion journals, you can start an animated discussion with just about any question on the right-hand page of each journal reading—especially "The Obvious" series of questions and "Exit Poll.")

Each session is followed by four or more "NEXTsheets"—reproducible pages of intriguing discussion starters, upbeat small-group activities, and hot lyrics of songs by Third Day, Buck, and the like. (The lyrics illustrate portions of the sessions.) You have permission to photocopy all NEXTsheets for use in your own youth group.

And don't think that *weekly* sessions are the only way to teach this curriculum. These four sessions fit perfectly into other programming, too—like a weeklong camp (one session per day) or a weekend retreat (two sessions per day).

This Leader's Guide is only one part of the *NEXT Level Youth Leader's Kit*, which makes the four-week curriculum you're holding now into a 30-day adventure for adolescent disciples. In the kit you get not only this Leader's Guide, but also six *NEXT Level Spiritual Challenge Journals* for students...a music CD from Benson that has some of today's edgiest Christian music and discipleship-driven lyrics (from Plankeye, Supertones, Out Of Eden, Buck, Jennifer Knapp, and more)...and a vibrant, energetic four-color promotional poster.

Well, that's about it. Read through these four sessions, prep your teachers or volunteers or small-group leaders—and go make disciples!

THE LEAST LIKELY TO SUCCEED

Most of Jesus' time on earth was spent confounding people's expectations. Almost everything he said and did came as a surprise to those around him. Case in point: his selection of disciples. Remember, this was a crucial decision. The people Jesus called to follow him would be responsible for continuing his work after his death and for starting his church.

The Pharisees and Sadducees, as arrogant as they were, probably would have been ideal candidates. They were educated and respected men. What's more, they had the political connections necessary to promote Jesus' social agenda.

Jesus, however, saw things differently. He opted for a group of tax collectors and fishermen, rogues and rascals who spent most of their three years with Jesus in a clueless fog. They weren't what you'd call obvious choices.

But Jesus saw beyond their rough exterior. He knew the kind of people he needed for the task at hand, and he chose them. And eventually, though it took some time, these men proved his judgment right.

The good news for us today is that the Lord continues to use unlikely people—even people like your group members—to accomplish his work.

Choose 'Em

Kick off your meeting with a game. Which game? *It doesn't matter!* Using the latest curriculum technology (at no extra cost to you, the consumer), we've come up with a meeting opener that works with any competition you can dream up. The only stipulation is that the game must involve at least two teams. Wanna try a Nerf basketball game? How about crab soccer? Maybe a balloon-on-a-tennis-racket relay race? Knock yourself out. This opener will work with all of them. If you're feeling especially democratic, you might even let your kids vote on which game *they'd* like to play.

How can one session accommodate such outrageous flexibility? Here's the secret: the key is not the game itself, but the way teams are chosen for the contest. Name yourself (or one of your fellow youth workers) as one of the team captains. Select one your kids—preferably someone who's hyper-competitive—to be the other captain. Then choose your teams, playground-style.

While your opponent stacks his team with the biggest, strongest, and fastest people in the group, you should put together a team of, well, less-obvious choices. Although your band of misfits may surprise their all-star opponents, the more likely scenario is that your team will get killed. That's okay.

To avoid reinforcing stereotypes and hurting the feelings of people likely to be chosen last for athletic competition, you could make the contest a cerebral activity. Bible baseball works for some groups. A pop-culture trivia quiz is also an option. You might even try a neutral contest like putting together a jigsaw puzzle in the shortest amount of time. In short, try reversing the pecking order of your group.

During the game, keep your eyes peeled for instances in which having the best (or most obviously desirable) players doesn't necessarily guarantee success. Use these examples to fuel the discussion that follows.

Acknowledge the captain of the winning team by saying something like, _____________ **knows how to pick a winning basketball** (or whatever) **team, but what if the choices weren't so obvious? What if someone came up to you and said, "We need you to be captain of a team that will start a church from scratch, one that will reach people of all ages in your neighborhood." The church would need to be started as soon as possible. Who would you choose to help you? Why?**

Though these questions would work well for small group discussion, you could also just have kids call out the names of people they would recruit for their church-planting teams. They may select people from your group, your church, your community, or the entire universe of living Christians. Write down the kids' suggestions on a whiteboard, poster board, or other writing surface. Ask volunteers to explain why they chose the people they did. Then, as a group, spend a minute or two trying to come up with common characteristics of the people on the list.

Jesus' Choices

Hand out copies of **The Stuff Disciples Are Made Of** (**NEXTsheet 1.1,** pages 11-12) and ask kids to work in pairs to complete the quiz. After a few minutes, read through the answers as a group. Pay attention to your kids' reactions to see if anyone is surprised by any of the answers. If so, use that surprise to introduce the next activity. Say something like this—

Here are the answers to **The Stuff Disciples Are Made Of:** 1. d; 2. a; 3. b; 4. d; 5. c; 6. a; 7. c; 8. a; 9. c; 10. a

People aren't always what they seem. That goes especially for the disciples. Even if you've never read the Bible in your life you've probably heard the names of disciples like Peter, John, and Paul. These guys are famous for their faith. Peter is said to be the first pope, for crying out loud! John and Paul wrote almost half of the New Testament—and that was before they hooked up with George and Ringo! A lot of people refer to these guys as "heroes of the faith." But, like most people, these heroes had some skeletons in their closets.

Point out that to get an accurate, warts-and-all account of what the disciples were really like, you have to go to the first five books of the New Testament—the gospels of Matthew, Mark, Luke, and John, and the Book of Acts.

Have kids quickly form groups of three or four. Give each group an index card and a Bible passage. Group members should read the Bible passage and then write down a one-sentence description of the disciples based on that passage. Each description should begin with the words, "The disciples were..."

Here are some passages you can use. We've included some sample descriptions that you can use to prompt group members, if necessary.

- Mark 1:16-20 (The disciples were impulsive, ready to drop what they were doing at a moment's notice.)
- Luke 8:22-25 (The disciples were less than brave in the face of danger.)
- Matthew 17:14-21 (The disciples were no strangers to failure.)
- Mark 14:32-42 (The disciples were unreliable.)
- Acts 4:13 (The disciples were just regular guys.)

If you've got a large group or if the activity proves to be especially popular with your group, here are some more Bible passages for you to use, along with some sample descriptions.

- Luke 5:33 (The disciples were partiers.)
- Mark 10:35-37 (The disciples were occasionally self-centered.)
- Matthew 24:3 (The disciples were curious.)
- Matthew 27:62-64 (The disciples were looked down upon.)

As the groups share their answers, jot down the descriptions they come up with. Then, using these descriptions, put together a portrait of Jesus' disciples. Talk briefly about how this portrait differs from your kids' previous notions of what the disciples were like.

Do the Disciples Measure Up?
If you have time, compare the list of descriptions with the list of characteristics they brainstormed in the "Choose 'Em" section. See how closely the actual disciples match up with the kids' ideas of the kind of people who would be most valuable in building a church from scratch.

Looks Can Be Deceiving

Now that we've painted a picture of the disciples as the biggest bunch of losers this side of a Jerry Springer audience, it's time to balance the portrayal. Sure, the disciples were rough around the edges. They were unreliable, prone to failure, and often had trouble understanding heavenly teachings. But Jesus looked beyond their shortcomings; he saw what was *inside* of them.

This odd way of looking at people was not something the Lord picked up when he came to earth, though. Verses like 1 Samuel 16:7 suggest that he's been interested in people's hearts since back in the days of soon-to-be-king David.

1 Samuel 16:7
But the Lord said to Samuel, "Do not consider his appearance or his height, for I have rejected him. The Lord does not look at the things man looks at. Man looks at the outward appearance, but the Lord looks at the heart."

Bring with you to the meeting some items that reinforce the idea that appearance is not reality. You might use a book of optical-illusion puzzles or pictures of animals whose looks belie their true nature. After examining the items you bring in, ask kids to share examples of when they misjudged someone based on appearance or when they themselves were misjudged.

Ask for three pairs of volunteers to prepare and present three-minute productions. Here's how it works:

You'll assign each pair a Bible passage. Each pair will then have exactly three minutes to look up its passage and prepare a short skit to illustrate it for the rest of the group. Each skit should last no more than a minute.

Here are some passages you can use:

- Matthew 14:25-29 (Peter conquers his fear long enough to take a step of faith onto the Sea of Galilee.)
- John 18:3-11 (Peter pulls a sword to protect Jesus.)
- Acts 3:1-10 (Peter and John heal a crippled beggar.)

After the last pair has performed, see how long it takes your students to recognize that all three passages describe a disciple (specifically Peter) doing something extraordinary or demonstrating unusual faith. Briefly discuss whether this newfound facet of the disciples' personalities changes your kids' impressions of them.

The Jumbled Verse
Looking for a more enjoyable way to introduce 1 Samuel 16:7? Try a jumble. Make several photocopies of the last two sentences of the verse ("The Lord does not look at . . . the Lord looks at the heart"). Cut apart the words on each photocopy and put them in an envelope. Divide your group into teams, and give each team an envelope. The winning team is the first team that correctly pieces together its verse.

God's Odd Choices

Now comes the so-what portion of the lesson. Put it to your kids bluntly—

So the disciples weren't perfect. They had their good days and their bad days, just like everybody else. Who cares, right? That was 2,000 years ago. What difference does it make in our lives today?

Leave the question hanging until several kids have offered their opinions.

Keep the discussion going until someone suggests that God still uses "regular" people today.

Divide the kids into three groups for a quick brainstorming session to address the question of why God chooses to work through ordinary people. Prime the well for group discussion by tossing out questions like these—

- **Why doesn't God work like advertising agencies and use only beautiful, recognizable, or respected people to get his message across?**
- **Why does he often trust his work to ordinary folks?**
- **And why on earth does he use people who don't even have their own lives completely together?**

Give the group members a few minutes to kick their ideas back and forth. Then have representatives from each group share their ideas. You may be surprised at the raw wisdom in the responses you get.

Toss your Bible to someone nearby and have that person read 1 Corinthians 1:26-31 aloud. Then repeat your earlier question: **Why does God choose to work through ordinary people?** Discuss as a group the wisdom of God's plan. A "wise," "influential," and "noble" person—someone that others look up to—might be tempted to look around at the things God accomplished through her and say, "Look what *I've* done." A "foolish," "weak," and "lowly" person, on the other hand, would have no illusions about himself. He would look around at God's accomplishments and say, "That had to be God's doing, because there's no way I could have done it."

If you have an extra minute or two, ask a few kids to share their feelings about God's penchant for working in the lives of ordinary people. Try to get a sense of whether your group members recognize the implications of 1 Corinthians 1:26-31 in their own lives.

Ipecac-tivity
Looking for a tasteful, wholesome activity to help your kids recognize the foolishness of judging people (and things) based on appearance? Good luck finding one. In the meantime, here's an idea that rates about 8 on the Disgust-o-meter. Pick up a dozen or so cream-filled or jelly-filled doughnuts. Scoop out the cream or jelly and replace it with a less-traditional pastry filling like ketchup, mustard, or shaving cream. (While there are more disgusting fillings you could use, it would be irresponsible for us to list things like hand lotion, Vaseline, shampoo, or vegetable shortening.)

For the sake of your relationship with the church janitorial staff, you should probably have a hurling contingency plan in place for doughnut eaters with weak stomachs. Your goal, of course, is not to make kids sick, but to remind them that it's what's on the inside that counts—with doughnuts as well as people.

1 Corinthians 1:26-29, 31
Brothers, think of what you were when you were called. Not many of you were wise by human standards; not many were influential; not many were of noble birth. But God chose the foolish things of the world to shame the wise; God chose the weak things of the world to shame the strong. He chose the lowly things of this world and the despised things—and the things that are not—to nullify the things that are, so that no one may boast before him...Therefore, as it is written: "Let him who boasts boast in the Lord."

Wanted: Imperfect People

Have kids reassemble into the three groups they formed earlier. Hand out the three scenarios on **Potential Disciples** (**NEXTsheet 1.2, 1.3,** and **1.4,** pages 13-15), assigning one to each group. Give the groups a few minutes to answer these questions (which are also on the NEXTsheets):

- **What obstacles might prevent this person from becoming an effective disciple?**
- **In what ways could God use this person, shortcomings and all, to accomplish his work?**
- **What would you say to this person right now about his view of discipleship?**

After a few minutes ask each group to read its scenario and then share its

If you feel the need to provide an outlet for your kids' creativity, ask a pair from each group to present its responses in skit form, perhaps as a dialogue.

responses. Encourage the rest of your kids to respond either positively or negatively to the small group's answers. Then ask group members to rate the person in the scenario on a scale of 1 to 10, according to his discipleship potential.

As you wrap up the session, get personal with your kids—in an anonymous sort of way. Hand out index cards. Ask kids to write down two things about themselves that they believe might prevent (or at least hinder) them from being effective disciples. Taking a cue from the people in the scenarios they just read, kids might list character traits, personal problems, or past mistakes. Warn kids not to write their names on the cards. (You might even encourage them to disguise their handwriting if it will make them feel more comfortable about being candid.)

After a few minutes, collect the cards, shuffle them, and read some of the responses. Ask group members to rebut each potential obstacle in their best lawyerly fashion. For particularly troublesome obstacles, draw some comparisons to Jesus' New Testament disciples. After all, most mistakes pale next to Peter's colossal failure of denying Jesus three times in one night! And you wanna talk character issues? Paul's early life was spent persecuting Christians. Yet God still worked mightily in and through the lives of these men.

Tune Time

If you'd prefer to wrap up the session with some tunes, try this. Hand out copies of the lyrics to "Who I Am" by Third Day (**NEXTsheet 1.5,** page 16) and "Unmade" by Massivivid (**NEXTsheet 1.6,** page 17); then play the songs from the CD. Encourage your kids to pay attention to the lyrics, particularly lines like, "Do You know who I am/Have You seen the things I've done" (from "Who I Am") and "You look into my skin and pull me inside out" (from "Unmade").

After the songs, briefly explore—

- How God works in the lives of ordinary, problem-plagued people
- How disciples can maintain a realistic view of their shortcomings and weaknesses without developing a negative self-image
- How people become disciples.

The Stuff Disciples Are Made Of

How much do you know about Jesus' closest friends, the people he handpicked to work with him during (and following) his time on earth? Take this quiz, and find out what the disciples were *really* like.

1. Why did Peter tell Jesus to get away from him when he first met the Lord? (Luke 5:8-9)

A. Jesus had just healed a leper, and Peter was afraid Jesus was contagious.
B. He mistook Jesus for a beggar.
C. After serving as a disciple of John the Baptist for three years, Peter wasn't ready to start following teachers around again.
D. Peter was ashamed of himself.

2. What did the disciples do when people brought their children to see Jesus? (Luke 18:15)

A. They yelled at the kids' parents, saying Jesus was too busy for such nonsense.
B. They thoughtlessly pushed aside crippled men and women to make way for the children.
C. They missed Jesus' parable of the mustard seed because they were too busy entertaining the little ones.
D. They charged half-price for all kids under the age of 12.

3. What problem did the Pharisees have with Jesus' disciples? (Luke 5:33)

A. They were bothered by the fish smell that lingered for days in the temple after the disciples worshipped there.
B. They thought the disciples partied too hard and too often.
C. They were offended that the disciples would not bow their heads when the chief priest walked by.
D. They resented the fact that the disciples referred to Jesus as "the wisest man in all of Israel."

4. How did the disciples respond after Jesus finished his parable of the seeds? (Luke 8:4-9)

A. They were so inspired by Jesus' words that they left immediately for Samaria to sow their own seeds of the Kingdom of God.
B. They took Jesus' words too literally and planted almost an entire garden before Jesus corrected them.
C. They got angry because the rest of the crowd didn't seem to understand the true meaning of the parable.
D. They asked Jesus what the heck he was talking about.

(over)

WWJD NEXT WWJD NEXT

5. What did Jesus do on the Sea of Galilee that scared the bejabbers out of his disciples? (John 6:16-21)

A. He kept making the "da-dum, da-dum, da-dum" sound from *Jaws*.
B. He told them each how and when they would die.
C. He took a stroll across the water.
D. He called down an army of 10,000 angels to show the disciples his power.

6. What frequent argument got the disciples in trouble? (Mark 10:35-37; Luke 9:46; 22:24)

A. Which of them would be the greatest in heaven.
B. Which of them had given up the most to follow Jesus.
C. Which of them was most popular with the lady disciples.
D. Which of them was the first to call Jesus "Lord."

7. When Peter told Jesus that he would not allow Jesus to be killed, how did Jesus respond? (Matthew 16:21-23)

A. He patiently explained to Peter (again) why he had to give his life to save the world.
B. He secretly told the rest of the disciples that Peter would be crucified as well.
C. He called Peter "Satan" and told him he was being a stumbling block.
D. He pointed out that Peter's *spirit* was willing to protect him, but that his *flesh* (or body) was weak.

8. On the night of his arrest, when Jesus needed the support of his closest friends, what did Peter, James, and John do for him? (Matthew 26:36-46)

A. They slept, for the most part, leaving Jesus to suffer alone.
B. They asked Jesus to teach them to pray so that they could provide the support he needed.
C. They cornered Judas Iscariot in a Jerusalem alley and beat the snot out of him.
D. They rented a room in Jerusalem, bought some bread and wine, and threw a fancy dinner party.

9. What did Peter do three times on the night of Jesus' arrest? (Luke 22:54-62)

A. He offered to take Jesus' place, even though it meant his own crucifixion.
B. He tried to collect bail money from the other disciples.
C. He lied about being one of Jesus' disciples in order to save his own skin.
D. He tried to sneak in to see Jesus.

10. Why didn't the disciples believe the women who told them Jesus' tomb was empty? (Luke 24:9-11)

A. The idea of someone rising from the dead seemed like nonsense to the disciples.
B. The women were giggling from excitement, which made it appear that they were making the story up.
C. The women kept mispronouncing Jesus' name.
D. The disciples had just returned from visiting Jesus' grave.

Potential Disciples

This is the story of Brittany, a young woman with the potential to be a great disciple. Unfortunately, Brittany hasn't recognized her potential yet. As you'll see, she's struggling with some serious obstacles in her life. Your job is to read Brittany's story and answer these three questions:

- What obstacles might prevent Brittany from becoming an effective disciple?
- In what ways could God use Brittany, shortcomings and all, to accomplish his work?
- What would you say to Brittany right now about her view of discipleship?

(As you answer the questions, assume that Brittany is a friend of yours.)

The Big Mistake

What a difference a year makes. Twelve months ago, Brittany was president of her youth group and a straight-A high school sophomore with plans to attend a Christian college. Then she met Phil. Swept up in a romance straight out of a Meg Ryan movie, Brittany and Phil began an intense love affair. A *very* intense love affair—one that included having sex.

For a while, Brittany managed to keep her sexual activity a secret from her parents, her friends, and her youth group. But when she got pregnant, everything hit the fan. Brittany's mother, in an effort to hide her daughter's "condition," sent Brittany to live with an aunt in Colorado. (Thanks to good ol' Phil, though, everyone at church and school knew what was really going on.)

Three months into the pregnancy, Brittany suffered a miscarriage. Still she decided to finish her junior year in Colorado. Now it was time to return home.

More than anything else, Brittany would love to go back to the way things were. She enjoyed her leadership role in the youth group. She liked encouraging others and pointing them to just the right Bible passage when they were hurting. She took her position as a role model seriously. But now all that's gone. How could anyone possibly take her seriously as a disciple of Jesus after what's happened?

Potential Disciples

This is the story of Michael, a young man with the potential to be a great disciple. Unfortunately, Michael hasn't recognized his potential yet. As you'll see, he's struggling with some serious obstacles in his life. Your job is to read Michael's story and answer these three questions:

- What obstacles might prevent Michael from becoming an effective disciple?
- In what ways could God use Michael, shortcomings and all, to accomplish his work?
- What would you say to Michael right now about his view of discipleship?

(As you answer the questions, assume that Michael is a friend of yours.)

Mr. Average

Michael's the type of guy who could blend into a crowd in a room by himself. Look up *nondescript* in the dictionary and you'll see Michael's picture next to it. Average height, average weight, average grades—there's just nothing about Michael that stands out. Through the years, he's learned to accept that about himself.

He's heard his youth leader talk about being a disciple, but figures discipleship is for other people. Michael reads the Bible, but doesn't understand a lot of it. One part that does make sense, though, is Jesus' miracle of feeding five thousand people with a couple fish and a few loaves of bread. Michael figures that if he'd been around in biblical times, he would have been one of those five thousand—a person interested enough in Jesus to follow him around, but not special enough to be one of his disciples. *Some people are just meant to be part of the crowd,* he figures. *Not everyone has to be a disciple.*

WWJD NEXT WWJD NEXT

WWJD NEXT WWJD NEXT

Potential Disciples

This is the story of Alejandro, a young man with the potential to be a great disciple. Unfortunately, Alejandro hasn't recognized his potential yet. As you'll see, he's struggling with some serious obstacles in his life. Your job is to read Alejandro's story and answer these three questions:

- What obstacles might prevent Alejandro from becoming an effective disciple?
- In what ways could God use Alejandro, shortcomings and all, to accomplish his work?
- What would you say to Alejandro right now about his view of discipleship?

(As you answer the questions, assume that Alejandro is a friend of yours.)

The Language Barrier

Alejandro's family immigrated to America over five years ago, and Alejandro still thinks of himself as an outsider. Though he learned English fairly quickly, Alejandro has had difficulty adjusting to things like American traditions, attitudes, and humor. He also speaks with an accent and is sometimes hard to understand. As a result, few people go out of their way to talk to or listen to him.

What's worse is that Alejandro actually has a lot to say. Unfortunately, though, he spends most of his time listening and watching. He sees the people at school who are hurting, lonely, and frustrated. He would love to tell them about the peace, comfort, and love that Jesus offers, but he doesn't dare. He knows the Bible, but he doesn't know how to talk to others about the things that are going on in their lives. Alejandro wonders if it's possible to be a silent disciple.

WWJD NEXT WWJD NEXT

Who I Am

performed by Third Day

I need to be someone who's a lot like You
Easy to see that I sure need something new
Though I try to live life my way, I think it goes to prove
That I need to be someone who's like You
And I know that You want to change me
Want to rearrange the way I feel inside
Yes, I've heard that You take
The broken hearts of lonely souls
And You make all things right

Do You know who I am?
Have You seen the things I've done?
Do You know who I am?
Have You seen the things I've done?

Never before, no, there's never been a time
That I would implore You to take what's Yours and mine
And to use it in the way You will
In any way You find
Never before did I realize
And I know that You want to change me
Want to rearrange the way I feel inside
Yes, I've heard that You take
The broken hearts of lonely souls
And You make all things right

Unmade

performed by Massivivid

I've no illusions who I am
This lightning shard of me
Cuts itself into reality
You look into my skin and pull me inside out
Right here in front of me . . . today
I'm running faster
Not in fear
But because my legs won't stop
You've broken me so fierce
I fear my sanity's been shattered
To a thousand tiny drops . . . today

And if You have the time
Won't You make nothing out of me
Would You be so kind
As to make nothing out of me

If I could speak weak enough to speak
The weakness of my soul
I'd cease to speak at all
Here is the holy ground
The Bush is burning now
But I dissolve . . . today

The cage is open now
You've pulled the doors and called to me
I want to be set free

Sitting Ducks

For many teenagers, the idea of outward discipleship runs completely counter to the survival techniques they've honed to a science. For them, surviving the high school years is a matter of camouflage, doing their best to blend in with the crowd. Their very real teenage insecurities prohibit them from doing anything that would draw unwanted attention.

Unfortunately, there's no such thing as an invisible disciple. If you're going to live your Christian faith, you're going to get noticed—and you might get ridiculed. To be a disciple is to be vulnerable.

Blindsided!

Start things off with Corridor Dodgeball. Put down two strips of masking tape, at least ten feet apart, to create a corridor in your meeting area. The corridor should run from wall to wall. Place a wastebasket or some other container at one end of the corridor. The only other equipment you'll need is a bunch of playground balls (one ball for every three people in the group is a good ratio).

Here's how the game works: One contestant, armed with a ball, starts out at the wall opposite the wastebasket. Everyone else lines both sides of the corridor, behind the tape. The rest of the balls are distributed randomly throughout the group.

The contestant must run to the opposite wall, drop his ball in the wastebasket, and run back—all the while dodging balls being thrown at him from both sides. While running to the wastebasket, he may use his ball to deflect those being thrown at him. On the way back, however, he has no protection. He must use only his dodging skills to avoid the balls.

To make the game a little fairer, you could make a rule that the people throwing the balls must do so in a chest-pass manner (both hands on the ball, pushing out from the chest), rather than in an overhand, baseball style. Even with this modification, though, most contestants should find the game difficult.

After the game, introduce the lesson topic by talking about how *vulnerable* your contestants felt without the ball to protect them. Discuss what it means to be vulnerable or susceptible to attack. Ask kids to talk about times when they've felt vulnerable.

If Corridor Dodgeball won't work in your meeting area, try a team game of Battleship. The only equipment you'll need is the classic board game Battleship (or if you're familiar with the rules, you can mark a 10-by-10 grid on large sheets of poster board with markers). Instead of using two players, however, you'll use two teams. Team members will confer before placing their ships on the board; then they'll take turns calling out locations, trying to sink the other team's ships. (Aside from the number of players, the rules of the game remain the same.)

After the winning team has been duly acknowledged, ask kids whether they've ever felt like the ships in the game, sitting ducks just waiting to be hit. Talk for a few minutes about how it feels to be vulnerable to verbal (and perhaps even physical) attacks.

Vulnerable and Uncomfortable

Hand out copies of **Actions and Reactions** (**NEXTsheet 2.1,** page 23). Give kids a few minutes to write down their responses. Afterward, split them up into three groups to talk about the sheet. Specifically, ask the members of each small group to determine which two or three actions scored highest and lowest on their comfort scales. Then let them mull over the question of why some of the things on the sheet are easier for them to do than others.

When you bring the entire group back together, briefly get feedback from the small groups. Then go through the sheet, asking group members to describe the worst-possible outcome of each action on the sheet. (But encourage kids to keep their answers grounded in reality, please. Any outcome that involves a shooting spree or a prison sentence is probably a little overboard.) For example, holding hands and praying at See You at the Pole (#4) could leave a person open to taunts of being gay. Defending creation in science class (#9) could cause a person to look like an idiot.

You're going to be using groups quite a bit during this session, so you may want to take a minute or two to think about how to split the kids up. While it would be nice to have a cross-section of different cliques in each small group, you want to make sure that you match up people who are comfortable with each other, people who can share openly with each other. Let each group choose a name for itself, and then use that name for the rest of the session.

Rather than just discussing these worst-case scenarios, why not have a few volunteers act them out for the group? They may either use group suggestions for their skits or come up with their own ideas.

Toss out some of the following questions to bring the issue closer to home:

- **How many of the things on this list have you ever done? How did they turn out? Did you catch any flak for them? If so, what happened? Which of them would you do again?**
- **What are some other ways in which a person might show her love for Christ publicly?**
- **Do you think there's anything wrong with being a silent Christian—someone who loves the Lord in his heart, but does nothing to demonstrate his faith to others? Explain your answer.**
- **Why do you suppose more people aren't open about their faith?**

Chances are, your conversation will circle the subject, but if no one mentions it, suggest that when we begin to demonstrate our faith, to live as Jesus instructed his disciples to live, we leave ourselves vulnerable to the attacks of others. Usually these attacks come in the form of taunts and teasing, being shunned or labeled a freak or fanatic.

Persecution Profiles

Say something like this—

So now we know: disciples are vulnerable. If you're going to associate yourself with Jesus, you might as well draw a big bull's eye on your back because people are going to take shots at you. We need to ask ourselves why that's the case.

Write two questions on the board:

- **Why do disciples get attacked when they're trying to do what's right?**
- **What causes people to want to take down someone with a heart for God?**

Divide kids into the small groups you organized earlier. Give them a few minutes to discuss and respond to these questions.

When you bring everyone back together, create an "enemy" profile, using the groups' responses. Write this on the board: "A person who attacks disciples..." Then rephrase the groups' responses to finish the sentence. Here are some examples:

A person who attacks disciples...

- *may think disciples act like they're better than everybody else.*
- *is usually just trying to get laughs.*
- *may be insecure about her own life.*

Briefly discuss the profile you come up with before taking the discussion to a more personal level. Say—

All right, here's a tough question for you. Be honest. Have you or your friends ever made fun of someone for doing what's right? Maybe you called her a brown-noser. Maybe you made jokes about the fact that he's saving sex for marriage. Maybe you said something as simple as "Get a life." Does any of that sound familiar?

Lead by example here. If you've been guilty of such things, spill the beans. Open up to your group by sharing what you said, why you said it, how your comments were received, and how you feel about them now.

Encourage your kids to share honestly. Chances are most of them will have stories similar to yours. The best way to figure out why people attack others who are trying to do what's right is to examine the times when we ourselves have been guilty of it.

Blessed Victims

Introduce the Bible study portion of the lesson this way: **Hey, do you guys wanna see a really scary Bible verse—a verse that might even change the way you think about God?** Now who could resist such a build up, right? Your kids will probably be leaping from their seats in anticipation, waiting for you to reveal the dreaded verse.

Hand your Bible to the person closest to you and have him pass it to the person next to him. Instruct the group to continue passing the Bible around while you close your eyes and count to ten. When you reach ten, have the person holding the Bible read Matthew 5:11 aloud.

Matthew 5:11
"Blessed are you when people insult you, persecute you and falsely say all kind of evil against you because of me."

See if your group members pick up on what's scary about the verse. If you need to, say something like this—

If I didn't know better, I'd say it almost seems like Jesus *wants* us to be attacked for following him. He says those who are insulted and persecuted because of their faith in him are *blessed*—almost as though that were his plan for us. But that doesn't make sense, does it? Why would Jesus want his disciples to be made fun of?

Let kids toss out their ideas, but don't help them. You want them to wrestle with this issue for a while.

Split the kids up into their small groups again. Hand out copies of **The Bible Tells Me So** (**NEXTsheet 2.2,** page 24), assigning one section to each group. Instruct each group to read its passage and answer the accompanying questions. After a few minutes, bring everyone together and have the groups share their findings.

Here are the Bible references and questions from the sheet:

Isaiah 55:8-9

- How might this passage comfort or reassure you when you're being insulted or made fun of for your beliefs?
- How can you tell the difference between God's ways and human ways?
- How could you explain this passage to a non-Christian friend without sounding conceited?

John 6:66-68

- How might this passage comfort or reassure you when you're being insulted or made fun of for your beliefs?
- Why do you suppose the disciples mentioned in verse 66 stopped following Jesus?
- How would you explain Peter's confession to a non-Christian friend?

2 Corinthians 6:14-16

- How might this passage comfort or reassure you when you're being insulted or made fun of for your beliefs?
- What kind of relationship should Christians have with unbelievers?
- How would you explain this passage to a non-Christian friend?

Summarize the Bible passages by pointing out that disciples and unbelievers live two different existences, with two different sets of values, two different sets of goals, and two different sets of priorities. When you get down to it, disciples and unbelievers have very little in common. In a sense, being insulted or persecuted is like a measuring stick for disciples. The further away we are from an unbeliever's comfort zone, the closer we are to God's ways. So if we're being attacked because of our faith, we know we must be causing the unbelievers some discomfort. On the other hand, if nobody notices our faith, it may mean that we're blending in with unbelievers a little too well.

The handout sheet includes the full Scripture passages as well as the questions. If you want your kids to look up and read the passages from their own Bibles, simply mask the passages when you photocopy the sheets.

Who's Got Your Back?

As you begin to wrap up the session, say something like—

So far we've talked about why people attack disciples and what the Bible has to say about it. Now let's focus on something a little more practical, like what kind of help we can expect when we're in the midst of an attack!

Acknowledge that the Bible and prayer are two very helpful tools for any disciple who's facing a tough time. Then explain that there's one other extremely helpful resource—and it's located somewhere in your meeting area! Give kids a minute or two to look around the room.

If they can't figure it out, demonstrate it for them. Have kids set up to play Corridor Dodgeball again. This time, however, modify the game slightly. The contestant will still be trying to put her ball in the wastebasket and get back without getting hit. This time, however, she will be accompanied by two teammates, each with a ball, who will protect her by deflecting thrown balls away from her.

After a couple of rounds, ask group members if they've figured out that the other helpful resource—disciples! Point out that the Bible tells us insults and persecution are part of the Lord's plans for his followers. Nowhere, however, does the Bible say that disciples have to face persecution alone!

Have someone read Ecclesiastes 4:9-12. Then, as a group, brainstorm a list of ways in which your kids can help support each other and deal with the insults and persecution that come with being a disciple.

To end the session, encourage your group members to commit themselves to being vulnerable together as disciples.

Ecclesiastes 4:9-12
Two are better than one, because they have a good return for their work: If one falls down, his friend can help him up. But pity the man who falls and has no one to help him up! Also, if two lie down together, they will keep warm. But how can one keep warm alone? Though one may be overpowered, two can defend themselves. A cord of three strands is not quickly broken.

When's the last time you tried a craft project with your group? Why not try one for this lesson? Bring in a bunch of art supplies (like paper, pencils, markers, crayons, scissors, glue, and glitter) and raw material (like magazines, cloth, and any weird odds and ends you can get your hands on). The only stipulations of the project are that the kids not ruin the carpet in your meeting area and that they create something that will serve as a reminder of this lesson. If some people have a hard time tapping into their creative juices, throw out some ideas. For example, someone might create a card that says, "I've got your back," and then have everyone in the group sign it. Another person might cut out words and letters from magazines to spell out the phrase "Vulnerable Together."

Tune Search
This can be done in small groups, or within the larger group. Explain to your kids that you'll be playing the Three Crosses song "I've Been Called," and their job is to listen to the lyrics and write down each line or phrase that has to do with the topic of this session—disciples being vulnerable, especially to the attacks of others (lyrics like "I know you never said / This would be easy" and "I may question / All the trials that I go through").

In you want, you can duplicate the song's lyrics (see **NEXTsheet 2.3,** page 25) for your students to follow along as they listen.

Then, in small groups or in the larger group, briefly discuss what they listed—and if you have the desire and time, extend the discussion to include other aspects of the song (God's call on a life, walking by faith instead of by sight, etc.).

Actions and Reactions

Below you'll find a list of ten things that might make a person vulnerable to being made fun of. Rate each one according to how comfortable you would feel doing it. Here's the scale:

5 = I'm totally cool with it—anytime, anywhere. Make fun of me all you want.
4 = I'd be comfortable with it until someone said something about it.
3 = I wouldn't do it myself, but I'd support someone else who did it.
2 = It just wouldn't be worth the hassle to me.
1 = Close the lid on my coffin, man, 'cause I'd rather die.

1. Wearing a W.W.J.D. bracelet (or some other accessory) — 1 2 3 4 5
2. Reading the Bible in study hall — 1 2 3 4 5
3. Giving a speech in English class about the "best decision you ever made"—giving your life to Christ — 1 2 3 4 5
4. Holding hands and praying around a flagpole during See You at the Pole — 1 2 3 4 5
5. Inviting someone you barely know to come to youth group with you — 1 2 3 4 5
6. Honking your horn—with a bunch of your friends in the car—when you see a bumper sticker that reads, "Honk if You Love Jesus" — 1 2 3 4 5
7. Appearing before the school board to ask for permission to start an after-school Bible study — 1 2 3 4 5
8. Telling a non-Christian friend that you're praying for him — 1 2 3 4 5
9. Explaining to your science teacher—in front of the whole class—why you believe in creation instead of evolution — 1 2 3 4 5
10. Striking up a conversation about God with a total stranger — 1 2 3 4 5

The Bible Tells Me So

Read your assigned passage and then answer the questions that follow.

"For my thoughts are not your thoughts, neither are your ways my ways," declares the Lord. "As the heavens are higher than the earth, so are my ways higher than your ways and my thoughts than your thoughts."

—Isaiah 55:8-9

- How might this passage comfort or reassure you when you're being insulted or made fun of for your beliefs?
- How can you tell the difference between God's ways and human ways?
- How could you explain this passage to a non-Christian friend without sounding conceited?

From this time many of his disciples turned back and no longer followed him.
"You do not want to leave, too, do you?" Jesus asked the Twelve.
Simon Peter answered him, "Lord, to whom shall we go? You have the words of eternal life."

—John 6:66-68

- How might this passage comfort or reassure you when you're being insulted or made fun of for your beliefs?
- Why do you suppose the disciples mentioned in verse 66 stopped following Jesus?
- How would you explain Peter's confession to a non-Christian friend?

Do not be yoked together with unbelievers. For what do righteousness and wickedness have in common? Or what fellowship can light have with darkness? What harmony is there between Christ and Belial? What does a believer have in common with an unbeliever? What agreement is there between the temple of God and idols? For we are the temple of the living God. As God has said: "I will live with them and walk among them, and I will be their God and they will be my people."

—2 Corinthians 6:14-16

- How might this passage comfort or reassure you when you're being insulted or made fun of for your beliefs?
- What kind of relationship should Christians have with unbelievers?
- How would you explain this passage to a non-Christian friend?

WWJD NEXT WWJD NEXT

I've Been Called

performed by Three Crosses

Father, You don't need a man like me
To sing Your praises
But still You let me sing
And surely You don't need
a man like me
I am not worthy
To fulfill Your smallest deed
Lately I've been thinking about my life
And how You changed me
Now You've made it all so clear to me

That I've been called to
serve You, Father
I've been called to give my life to You
And that's all I need to know
I understand, I finally understand
I'm part of Your plan

Father, I know You never said
This would be easy
But Your grace will be my strength
You know, some days it's hard to see
How this mountain I must climb
Will bring You close to me
And Lord, I may question
All the trials that I go through
But Lord, I'll never question You, 'cause

I've been called to serve You, Father
I've been called to give my life to You
And that's all I need to know
I understand, I finally understand

I'm gonna take some time
Leave this world behind me
I'm gonna take some time
Down on my knees with You

Father, I can't see what Your eyes see
But I don't need to
So I will walk by faith
I know I may never comprehend
My life's purpose
But I know that in the end

I've been called to serve You, Father
I've been called to give my life to You
And that's all I need to now
I understand I'm part of Your plan
I've been called

Jewish Messiah Seeking Committed, Long-Term Relationship

Jesus wasn't what you'd call a dabbler or a halfway kind of guy. He didn't say that if your eye causes you to sin, you should close it for a while. He said yank the eyeball out and throw it away. He didn't stand around complaining about the merchants who had invaded the temple. He went in and kicked some money-changing booty. He didn't come to just *tell* us about salvation. He gave himself to be tortured and killed in order to provide that salvation.

It's no surprise, then, that the Lord's not much interested in halfway disciples. Dabblers need not apply. Jesus didn't say, "Come, listen to my teachings." He said, "Drop everything and follow me." That same invitation stands today. To be a disciple of Jesus is to be totally committed to him. It requires us to arrange our priorities around his plans for our lives. It requires us to focus on his will, often to the exclusion of things that other people consider important.

Lead, Follow, or Don't Play

Begin the session with the classic children's game Follow the Leader. With just the slightest bit of prompting, you'll have your kids following you merrily around the room, skipping and singing and—

Follow the stinking leader?! you're probably saying to yourself. *That's your idea of a meeting opener? My kids wouldn't follow me out of a burning building! There's no way they're going to play follow the leader—unless you throw one of those wacky, unexpected twists into the game and maybe offer them a bribe.*

Okay, okay—here's the obligatory twist: You'll be using five different leaders. (Recruit other staff members—and a few kids, if necessary—to be leaders.) Most of the rules for regular Follow the Leader apply. That is, players will line up behind a leader and go everywhere he goes, doing everything he does. First, though, they will have to decide which of the five leaders they want to follow.

You can play this up as much as you want. Each leader might try to recruit followers using different persuasion techniques. One might try ordering people around like a drill sergeant. Another might try sweet talk. Still another might remain completely silent.

Choosing the right leader, though, will prove to be important. You see, one of the five will lead his group to a stash of mini-candy bars. (Call it a bribe if you must; we prefer the term *prize.*). The rest will lead their groups to various dead ends around the building. Once players have chosen a leader to follow, they cannot change their minds.

You'll need to talk briefly with your leaders before the game to determine who goes where. Encourage them to be creative and more than a little goofy in their actions.

After the game, ask players to explain why they chose to commit themselves to a certain leader. Use the activity to lead into a discussion of what it means to be committed to someone or something.

So, Follow the Leader isn't disgusting or messy enough for you? Try an extreme treasure hunt. Before the game, hide written clues (sealed in envelopes) in weird places around your meeting area. Each clue should lead hunters to the location of the next clue.

What makes the treasure hunt extreme, though, are the places you hide the clues and the manner in which kids must retrieve them. For example, one clue might be buried in sand and may only be retrieved by a player's toes. Another might be hidden at the bottom of a bowl of pudding and may be retrieved only by a player's teeth. Another might be hung from a string above a filled baptismal. The possibilities are limited only by your good taste and the ire of the church janitorial staff.

The idea is that players must really commit themselves to the treasure hunt in order to win. Use that hook to introduce the topic of commitment.

Distraction Attraction

Ask group members to call out some things they are committed to. Emphasize that not all of the responses have to be serious. Each time someone calls out a response, have her also name some things that get in the way of that commitment.

For example, if one of your party animals says she's committed to having a good time, ask her to name some things that get in the way of having a good time. She may list things like school, parents, cops, and so on.

If one of your jocks says he's committed to football, have him list some things that might interfere with his commitment. He might name things like injuries, school work, and unsympathetic coaches.

If some sweethearts in your group say they're committed to each other, you may need to ask the rest of the group to name some things that might interfere with their commitment. Your group will probably accommodate you with suggestions like other people, college, and disapproving parents.

For now, put off anyone who mentions a spiritual commitment. Explain that you'll be discussing that later in the meeting.

Put this question to the group: **If a person is *truly* committed to something, do you think it's possible for him to be distracted from it?** Don't allow any easy answers here. Make your kids put some thought into the questions before they answer. Some may say that all people, no matter how committed they are, get distracted sometimes. Others may counter by saying that if a person is able to be distracted, she probably wasn't committed to begin with. If you get two differing opinions, you might consider staging a brief, impromptu debate.

Before you move on to the Bible study, make sure that you and your kids are on the same page. Ask several of them to talk briefly about their ideas of commitment. What is it? How can you tell if someone is committed to something?

Looking for a more active way to introduce the ideas of commitment and distraction? Divide the group in half. Give half the group some kind of a timed assignment—like building a house of cards, making a Lego structure, or completing a jigsaw puzzle. Secretly inform the kids in the other half of the group that their responsibility is to prevent the other group from completing its assignment. Their weapon is distraction. They may use conversation, flirting, humor, or (almost) anything else short of physical contact as distractions.

After time is up, discuss which distractions were most effective and which were least effective. Use the activity to lead into a discussion of the things that distract us from our commitment as disciples.

Holy Hatred?

Introduce the Bible study by pointing out that Jesus had some pretty surprising things to say about commitment and discipleship. Divide kids into two groups. Hand out copies of **Tales of Extreme Commitment** (**NEXTsheet 3.1,** page 30) and assign one section of the sheet to each group. Instruct the groups to read their assigned passage and answer the questions that follow.

For your convenience, here are the Bible references and questions from the sheet:

Matthew 10:37

- How would you explain this verse to a family member who's not a Christian?
- What can we learn about a disciple's priorities from this verse?
- Why do you suppose Jesus demands such a strict commitment from his followers?

Luke 14:26

- How would you explain this verse to a family member who's not a Christian?
- What can we learn about a disciple's priorities from this verse?
- Why do you suppose Jesus demands such a strict commitment from his followers?

The handout sheet includes the full Scripture passages as well as the questions. If you want your kids to look up and read the passages from their own Bibles, simply mask the passages when you photocopy the sheets.

Make sure your kids are clear about what Jesus is saying in these verses. (The last thing many of them need is a biblical mandate to hate their parents.) Point out that it's a matter of comparison. Of course, we should love our parents. But compared to the love we have for Jesus, that love should seem like hate. As Christians and disciples of Jesus, our first and deepest commitment should be to him.

Self-Exam

Hand out copies of **So Many Distractions, So Little Time** (**NEXTsheet 3.2**, page 31). Give kids a few minutes to fill out the sheet. When they're finished, have them pair up to discuss their responses.

Throw out some of the following questions for the pairs to talk over:

- **On a scale of 1 to 10, how would you rate your overall commitment as a disciple?**
- **Explain why you didn't give yourself a higher rating.**
- **On a scale of 1 to 10, how easily distracted are you when it comes to your discipleship commitment?**
- **Look at the distraction that you rated highest on your list. Why do you think that person or activity is so distracting to you?**

Encourage kids to be honest with themselves and then share honestly with their partners. In a perfect world, you might see some informal accountability relationships develop as a result of this discussion. Of course, you want to do everything possible to encourage such relationships.

As you wrap up the session, split up the pairs and hand out index cards. Give your kids a few minutes to think about what they can do to strengthen their commitment as disciples. Suggest that a logical first step would be to identify the number-one distraction in one's life and then come up with, say, a three-point strategy for lessening the pull of that distraction.

For example, let's say a girl in your group identified her boyfriend as her biggest distraction. Here are three things she might do to lessen his distracting influence in her life:

1. Cut her weekly phone time with him in half and increase her quiet time.
2. Insist that once a month they participate in a service project together.
3. Establish one no-talk, no-see evening a week, whether it be Sunday night or youth group night.

Note that these strategies do not necessarily involve eliminating the distraction from one's life. Often a simple restructuring of priorities and a keener awareness of time spent will go a long way toward correcting the problem.

In closing, encourage your kids to hang on to their index cards and put them in a place where they'll be seen throughout the week. Make yourself available to anyone who'd like to talk about discipleship commitment or the distractions in his life.

Song of the Night

Divide the group in two—males and females, upperclassmen and underclassmen, whatever. Make sure each group has a tape or CD player. Give one group a recording of "Next" by Buck, along with the lyrics to the song (**NEXTsheet 3.3,** page 32). Give the other group a recording of "If We Were Lovers" by All Star United, along with the song's lyrics (**NEXTsheet 3.4,** page 33).

Say: **Here's what you're gonna do. Listen to your song a couple times, read the lyrics, and then come up with some reasons why your song should be named the official theme song of this meeting. Remember, we're talking about commitment and distraction, so make sure your list of reasons includes something about those topics.**

Recruit an impartial judge (maybe a volunteer worker or someone passing in the hall) to listen to the groups' presentations and determine which song deserves to be named the meeting's theme song. Play the winning song at the end of your meeting.

WWJD NEXT WWJD NEXT

Tales of Extreme Commitment

Step One: Read your assigned verse.
Step Two: Answer the questions that follow the verse.
Step Three: Rewrite the verse in its original Greek language.
Step Four: Conjugate each verb in the verse.
Step Five: Ignore steps three and four.

"Anyone who loves his father or mother more than me is not worthy of me; anyone who loves his son or daughter more than me is not worthy of me."

—Matthew 10:37

- How would you explain this verse to a family member who's not a Christian?
- What can we learn about a disciple's priorities from this verse?
- Why do you suppose Jesus demands such a strict commitment from his followers?

"If anyone comes to me and does not hate his father and mother, his wife and children, his brothers and sisters—yes, even his own life—he cannot be my disciple.

—Luke 14:26

- How would you explain this verse to a family member who's not a Christian?
- What can we learn about a disciple's priorities from this verse?
- Why do you suppose Jesus demands such a strict commitment from his followers?

So Many Distractions, So Little Time

This is a list of potential distractions, people and things that could interfere with a disciple's commitment. It's also a personal checklist for you.

- First, fill in the blanks with any other distractions we forgot to mention.
- Next, go through the list and cross out any items that don't apply to you.
- Finally, rank the remaining items based on how distracting they are to you personally. Write "1" next to your biggest distraction, "2" next to your second biggest, and so on.

____ **Boyfriend/girlfriend**

____ **Parents**

____ **Sports**

____ **TV**

____ **Friends**

____ **Music**

____ **Computer/video games**

____ **Surfing the Net**

____ **Band**

____ **Brothers/sisters**

____ **Cruising**

____ **Hanging out at the mall**

____ **Sleeping**

____ **Going to clubs**

____ **Other:**

____ **Other:**

WWJD NEXT WWJD NEXT

Next

Performed by Buck

Lately I've been thinking about
the games I play
And how He gave Himself away
And what that means to me
Lately I've been dreaming about
the way He loved
And the way He suffered for
A wounded world that won't believe
Sometimes I'm ashamed about
the things I say
And the things I see me do
And how they seem so far removed
Sometimes I hang my head
like the walking dead
When I dare to ask myself
What would Jesus really do

He is alive in us
Jesus loves the hurting ones

What's next?
Reaching hands out to the helpless
Fill pockets of the poor
What's next?
Giving mercy to the sinner
Forgiving a little more
What's next?
Touching those untouchable
Healing the leper's sore
What's next?
Loving those unlovable
Or what is love good for

I've come to understand we are His hands
His goodness and His light
To the hopeless and despised
Now I've come to realize that the love of
Christ is so much more than words
We are a living sacrifice

He is alive in us
Jesus loves the hurting ones

What's next?
Reaching hands out to the helpless
Fill pockets of the poor
What's next?
Giving mercy to the sinner
Forgiving a little more
What's next?
Touching those untouchable
Healing the leper's sore
What's next?
Loving those unlovable
Or what's love good for

Love is what is—love is what's next
Love is what is—love is next
Love is what is—love is what's next
Love is
Love is
Love is what's

What's next?
Reaching hands out to the helpless
Fill pockets of the poor
What's next?
Giving mercy to the sinner
Forgiving a little more
What's next?
Touching those untouchable
Healing the leper's sore
What's next?
Loving those unlovable
Or what's love good for

If We Were Lovers

performed by All Star United

Let's talk a walk
Into the sky
Conversing with the stars
To fathom why
They're not afraid to burn
To lose themselves
While turning into light

If we were lovers
Like we were meant to be
Open arms, broken hearts
All the world to see
If we were lovers
Loving like we say
Oh, the ghosts of doubt
Would crash and burn away
If we were lovers

The obvious
Will be implied
From the simple implications of
our lives
If we don't get it right
I guess they're going to wait
a long, long time

If we were lovers
Like we were meant to be
Open arms, broken hearts
All the world to see
If we were lovers
Loving like we say
Oh the ghosts of doubt
Would crash and burn away

An extraordinary love
Offers heal for hurt,
and kind for cruelty
Words are not enough
Revolution might begin with
you and me

If we were lovers
If we were lovers
If we were lovers
If we were lovers
If we were lovers
If we were lovers
Then we would love

NO GUTS, NO GLORY

Sometimes we underestimate just how much courage it takes for teenagers to be open about their faith. The Discovery Channel host who claimed that crocodiles are the only animals on earth that prey on human beings obviously doesn't remember his high school days. Teenagers can be vicious creatures, especially when an outsider threatens the balance of their herd mentality.

Jesus instructs his disciples to let their light shine constantly, to be bold and up-front about their relationship with him, regardless of the consequences. It takes guts to be a disciple, a thought that is at once both affirming and unsettling.

Drink Up(chuck)

Since the topic of this session is boldness or gutsiness, try starting things off with a test of courage. The game of Guts is played every day in school cafeterias everywhere. Preparation for the game is relatively simple. Clear out your refrigerator, your spice rack, and your pantry. Put the contents in a cooler and bring them to the meeting. You'll also need a large glass pitcher and a stirring spoon.

Start the game by pouring some milk into the pitcher. Then ask your group: **How many of you have the guts to drink what's in here?** All but the lactose intolerant will probably raise their hands.

Add some chocolate syrup to the milk and repeat your question. Again, most students will probably raise their hands.

Continue adding ingredients to the mix one at a time. After each ingredient is added, check to see how many kids would still be willing to drink it. As the game progresses, the ingredients you add should be less and less appetizing. For example, peanut butter might be followed by cream cheese, a raw egg, pickle relish, and canned peas. Keep stirring the slop to achieve a properly disgusting consistency.

The game continues until only one hearty, courageous, twisted player remains. Declare this person to be the group member with the most guts. (For an ironic ending to the game, don't even make the winner drink the mixture.)

Believe it or not, this sick opener will dovetail nicely into a discussion of discipleship. Point out that in the beginning discipleship is pretty easy. It's just a matter of making a commitment to the Lord. Most Christians would have no problem with that idea—just as most of your kids had no problem with the idea of drinking the plain milk.

As things progress, though, people find that there's more to discipleship than they might have expected—helping hurting people, maintaining an active prayer life, studying God's Word. At this point discipleship becomes less appetizing for some. Throw in things like insults, persecution, and rejection, and you'll come to the conclusion that it takes a seriously gutsy person to be an active disciple of Jesus.

Want a more active opener? Capture the Flag (or any variation that calls for kids to retrieve something from enemy territory) will work well. Keep your eyes peeled during the game for examples of bravery and boldness. Use these examples later to introduce the idea of being a gutsy disciple.

The Whole Truth and Nothing But

To get your kids talking openly about boldness and bravery, try a game of Truth or Dare. If you're unfamiliar with this slumber-party favorite, here's a brief overview. Point to a person in the group and ask, "**Truth or dare?**" If the person chooses truth, she must answer a question honestly—no matter what that question is. If she chooses dare, she has to do whatever you say.

Keep in mind that as youth group leader, you have the power to rig such an activity to fit your needs. For the purposes of this lesson, you're going to want kids to choose truth. To get them to do that, though, you'll need to come up with some dares that are seriously unappealing. (Toward that end, don't forget the food products you used earlier. When the alternative is smearing pickle relish in your hair, truthfully answering a question suddenly doesn't seem so bad.)

Here are some questions you can use for those who choose truth:

- **Who is the gutsiest person you know?**
- **What are you most afraid of?**
- **When was the last time someone made fun of you because of your faith?**
- **What's the boldest thing that you've ever done as a disciple?**
- **What keeps you from being a gutsier disciple?**
- **What's the most cowardly thing you've done as a disciple?**
- **When was the last time you could have taken a stand as a disciple, but didn't?**

If your kids seem reluctant to part with such personal information, lead the way for them by answering each question yourself first.

The Gutsy Disciple

Hand out copies of **A Friend in Need** (**NEXTsheet 4.1,** page 38). Let kids work in pairs to answer the questions. After a few minutes, find out what they came up with. Ask each pair one of the questions on the sheet as though you are the friend mentioned in the introduction. The members of each pair should respond to you as though they're talking to a friend.

Here are the questions from the sheet concerning Philippians 1:27-30:

- *Verse 27 says we're supposed to act in a way that's "worthy of the gospel of Christ." What does that mean? How do I know if what I'm doing is worthy of Christ?*
- *The word* contending *in verse 27 means* fighting *or* battling. *Does God really want*

us to fight for him? If so, how—and when?

- *Verse 28 says we shouldn't be frightened when people oppose us. But when people start arguing with me or say I'm wrong or a fanatic or something, I freak. I get real nervous. Does that mean I'm not a good disciple?*
- *Verse 29 says that "it has been granted us...to suffer for him"—like it's some kind of gift or something. What kind of a gift is that? Why does the Lord want us to suffer for him?*
- *What does this passage mean to you?*

If other pairs have something to add during a conversation, encourage them to chime in.

Before you wrap up the Bible study, throw out one final question to your group members: **Why do you suppose the Lord prefers his disciples to be bold and gutsy?** Get opinions from as many kids as you can.

Profiles in Courage
As a supplement to the Bible study, give your kids a glimpse of bold discipleship in action. The following passages spotlight some truly gutsy followers of Christ:
- Matthew 14:22-31 (Peter risks his life to walk on water with Jesus.)
- Acts 4:1-22 (Peter and John speak boldly before the Sanhedrin, knowing that the penalty may be death.)
- Acts 6:8-7:60 (Stephen pays with his life for talking about Christ.)
- Acts 21:37-22:21 (Paul risks his life to share his story of becoming a Christian.)

Bold Over...and Over

Have kids reassemble into the pairs they formed earlier. Hand out copies of **Courage Under Fire** (**NEXTsheet 4.2,** page 39). Give the pairs a few minutes to read through the situations and come up with an "easy" solution for each one, a solution that will result in the least amount of conflict, embarrassment, and problems. When everyone's finished, have each pair share (briefly) its easy solutions.

Then send the pairs back to the sheet for the second part of the assignment: imagining how a bold, gutsy disciple would respond in each situation. Give the pairs a little more time to come up with these responses. When they're finished, go through the situations one at a time, asking each pair to explain its response. Encourage discussion, questions, and objections among the pairs as these solutions are presented.

If you have time (and a willing participant), ask a volunteer from the group to share a recent personal experience that called for bold discipleship. Ask her to explain how she handled the situation. Then ask group members to suggest alternate ways that she might have handled it.

Read aloud Acts 4:13. Point out that Peter and John were ordinary people, just like us, who were capable of amazing acts of courage. Ask your group members to write this verse down somewhere as a reminder that they too are capable of amazing courage.

Acts 4:13
When they saw the courage of Peter and John and realized that they were unschooled, ordinary men, they were astonished and they took note that these men had been with Jesus.

Tune Interlude
Hand out copies of the lyrics to "The Spring" by Between Thieves (**NEXTsheet 4.3,** page 40), then play the song from the CD. Ask your students to listen carefully to the lyrics. Focus especially on lines like "Standing over the waterfall/Leaning over the edge/I fall into the spring that heals the wounds." Discuss briefly the courage it takes to finally turn one's life over to Jesus and become a committed disciple.

Unexpected Substitutions

Wrap up the session (and this study) with a simple affirmation exercise for your kids. The preparation for this exercise is minimal. All you'll need to do is put together a list of Scripture passages in which a disciple (or any follower of

Christ) is mentioned or portrayed in a positive light. Try to find at least one passage for every student in your group.

As you conclude the meeting, announce that you have some final Bible verses you'd like your kids to remember. When you read each passage, substitute the name of one of your group members for the disciple's name in the text. If you really want to get ambitious, you can substitute personal details as well.

For example, Matthew 4:18-20 might be read this way:

"As Jesus was walking past Melas Park, he saw two brothers, Robert called Robbie and his brother Kyle. They were shooting baskets, for they were basketball players. 'Come, follow me,' Jesus said, 'and I will show you how to score eternal points.' At once they left the court and followed him."

Of course, not all passages will lend themselves to such detail. Some, like 1 Timothy 1:2, may allow you to substitute only a name. That's okay. The key is to make sure that everyone in the group is mentioned in the context of a Scripture passage.

Here are some passages you can use:

- Matthew 14:25-29
- Matthew 16:15-17
- Luke 10:41-42
- 1 Timothy 6:20-21

When kids start to giggle or question you, ask them what's so strange about the passages you're reading. Point out that disciples haven't changed much in the past two thousand years. There's very little difference between the people mentioned in the Bible and people today. A bold disciple is a bold disciple in any age. Remind your group members that if God could use the people in Scripture to accomplish his work, he can certainly use us! God will always use a vulnerable, committed, and gutsy disciple.

Feeling ambitious? Why not close this study with a student-led worship service? Appoint one group of kids to take care of music for the service. Have another group schedule a speaker. Put another group in charge of announcements and Scripture reading. (Another option is to put a group in charge of communion at the end of the service.)

Explain to your group members that the elements of the service should all somehow relate to discipleship. Then leave everything else to them. You'll probably be pleasantly surprised at the worship event your kids come up with.

WWJD NEXT WWJD NEXT

A Friend in Need

One of your best friends has been struggling with his discipleship lately. The problem is his boldness and courage. He's the kind of guy who doesn't like to draw attention to himself. He tends to withdraw and keep quiet—even in conversations about Christianity. And if there's conflict or confrontation involved, forget about it. Your friend won't say a word.

He knows it's a problem, and he's come to you for help. He found an interesting passage in the Bible, but he has some questions about it. See if you can help him.

Whatever happens, conduct yourselves in a manner worthy of the gospel of Christ. Then, whether I come and see you or only hear about you in my absence, I will know that you stand firm in one spirit, contending as one man for the faith of the gospel without being frightened in any way by those who oppose you. This is a sign to them that they will be destroyed, but that you will be saved—and that by God. For it has been granted to you on behalf of Christ not only to believe on him, but also to suffer for him, since you are going through the same struggle you saw I had, and now hear that I still have.

—Philippians 1:27-30

- Verse 27 says we're supposed to act in a way that's "worthy of the gospel of Christ." What does that mean? How do I know if what I'm doing is worthy of Christ?

- The word *contending* in verse 27 means *fighting* or *battling*. Does God really want us to fight for him? If so, how—and when?

- Verse 28 says we shouldn't be frightened when people oppose us. But when people start arguing with me or say I'm wrong or a fanatic or something, I freak. I get real nervous. Does that mean I'm not a good disciple?

- Verse 29 says that "it has been granted us...to suffer for him"—like it's some kind of gift or something. What kind of a gift is that? Why does the Lord want us to suffer for him?

- What does this passage mean to you?

WWJD NEXT WWJD NEXT

Courage Under Fire

Below you'll find the stories of two young people like yourself—Ana and Cal. Both of them are committed Christians, disciples of Christ. What's more, both recently made commitments to be bolder and gutsier in their Christian walk. Now each is facing a situation that puts that commitment to the test.

Read through the situations twice. The first time through, think of the easiest possible solution for each situation, the one that will cause the least amount of conflict, embarrassment, and problems for the people involved. The second time through, think of how a bold, gutsy disciple would handle each situation.

• **Ana was sitting in the biology lab,** waiting for class to start, when Kim started in. "Have you ever seen those stupid T-shirts people wear that kind of look like real T-shirts, but have, like, Christian sayings on them?" Kim asked.

"Oh, yeah," Vonda chimed in, "they say stuff like 'God's Gym' and 'Big God' instead of 'Big Dog.'"

Rachel, one of Ana's former friends, smiled mischievously. She pointed at Ana and announced, "She goes to church. Why don't you ask her?"

Kim turned to Ana with a look of disgust. "Why do you guys wear stuff like that? Does your church make you do it so that people will know you're religious and stuff?"

Ana could hear Vonda and Rachel snicker behind her.

• **Cal had been dating Courtney for about two months** when he got the dreaded invitation: dinner at Courtney's on Friday night to meet the family. Cal had met Courtney's mom once or twice when he picked up Courtney for a date, but he'd never seen her dad, a city police officer.

When Cal arrived at Courtney's, he was greeted at the door by her father. "Courtney's in the kitchen helping her mom with dinner," Courtney's father explained. "I've got the Red Wings game on in the den. Let's go in there."

Cal tried to make some small talk about the Red Wings' chances this year, but Courtney's father seemed uninterested. After a minute or so of awkward silence, Courtney's dad leaned toward Cal and said in a low voice, "Did you ever hear the one about—" He then proceeded to rattle off three of the most disgusting, racially offensive jokes Cal had ever heard.

He was just about to start a fourth one when Courtney walked in. "Dad, you're not telling Cal dirty jokes, are you?"

"Hey, we're just a couple guys talking," her dad replied. "Right, Cal?" He turned to Cal for an answer, then added, "You're not one of those politically correct types who starts whining every time someone tells a harmless joke are you?"

The Spring

performed by Between Thieves

Gaze into the water
See a face I recognize no longer
Gone so far from who I am
Need to live beyond this life
Remove the veil of this disguise
Time to trust in You again

Standing over the waterfall
Leaning over the edge

Chorus
I fall into the spring that heals the wounds
Quench the thirst with heavenly glory
Feel the water rushing over me
Reveal the scars that tell the story

Gaze into the water
See a face that I despise no longer
Come so far from where I've been
Your image draws me nearer
Show me how to see you clearer
Savior, wash away my sin

Standing over the waterfall
In the light of the truth

Repeat chorus

Longing for perfection
When I see You in my own reflection
Thirsty to be sanctified
Now I come to You unworthy
Prince of Pardon, Lord of Mercy
In You I am baptized

RESOURCES FROM YOUTH SPECIALTIES

Professional Resources

Administration, Publicity, & Fundraising (Ideas Library)
Developing Student Leaders
Equipped to Serve: Volunteer Youth Worker Training Course
Help! I'm a Junior High Youth Worker!
Help! I'm a Small-Group Leader!
Help! I'm a Sunday School Teacher!
Help! I'm a Volunteer Youth Worker!
How to Expand Your Youth Ministry
How to Speak to Youth...and Keep Them Awake at the Same Time
Junior High Ministry (Updated & Expanded)
The Ministry of Nurture: A Youth Worker's Guide to Discipling Teenagers
One Kid at a Time: Reaching Youth through Mentoring
Purpose-Driven Youth Ministry
So *That's* Why I Keep Doing This! 52 Devotional Stories for Youth Workers
A Youth Ministry Crash Course
The Youth Worker's Handbook to Family Ministry

Youth Ministry Programming

Camps, Retreats, Missions, & Service Ideas (Ideas Library)
Compassionate Kids: Practical Ways to Involve Your Students in Mission and Service
Creative Bible Lessons from the Old Testament
Creative Bible Lessons in John: Encounters with Jesus
Creative Bible Lessons in Romans: Faith on Fire!
Creative Bible Lessons on the Life of Christ
Creative Junior High Programs from A to Z, Vol. 1 (A-M)
Creative Junior High Programs from A to Z, Vol. 2 (N-Z)
Creative Meetings, Bible Lessons, & Worship Ideas (Ideas Library)
Crowd Breakers & Mixers (Ideas Library)
Drama, Skits, & Sketches (Ideas Library)
Drama, Skits, & Sketches 2 (Ideas Library)
Dramatic Pauses
Everyday Object Lessons
Facing Your Future: Graduating Youth Group with a Faith That Lasts
Games (Ideas Library)
Games 2 (Ideas Library)
Great Fundraising Ideas for Youth Groups
More Great Fundraising Ideas for Youth Groups
Great Retreats for Youth Groups
Greatest Skits on Earth
Greatest Skits on Earth, Vol. 2
Holiday Ideas (Ideas Library)
Hot Illustrations for Youth Talks
More Hot Illustrations for Youth Talks
Still More Hot Illustrations for Youth Talks
Incredible Questionnaires for Youth Ministry
Junior High Game Nights
More Junior High Game Nights
Kickstarters: 101 Ingenious Intros to Just about Any Bible Lesson
Live the Life! Student Evangelism Training Kit
Memory Makers
Play It! Great Games for Groups
Play It Again! More Great Games for Groups
Special Events (Ideas Library)
Spontaneous Melodramas
Super Sketches for Youth Ministry
Teaching the Bible Creatively
What Would Jesus Do? Youth Leader's Kit
WWJD—The Next Level
Wild Truth Bible Lessons
Wild Truth Bible Lessons 2
Worship Services for Youth Groups

Discussion Starters

Discussion & Lesson Starters (Ideas Library)
Discussion & Lesson Starters 2 (Ideas Library)
Get 'Em Talking
Keep 'Em Talking!
High School TalkSheets
More High School TalkSheets
High School TalkSheets: Psalms and Proverbs
Junior High TalkSheets
More Junior High TalkSheets
Junior High TalkSheets: Psalms and Proverbs
What If...? 450 Thought-Provoking Questions to Get Teenagers Talking, Laughing, and Thinking
Would You Rather...? 465 Provocative Questions to Get Teenagers Talking
Have You Ever...? 450 Intriguing Questions Guaranteed to Get Teenagers Talking

Clip Art

ArtSource: Stark Raving Clip Art (print)
ArtSource CD-ROM: Ultimate Clip Art

Videos

EdgeTV
The Heart of Youth Ministry: A Morning with Mike Yaconelli
Next Time I Fall in Love Video Curriculum
Understanding Your Teenager Video Curriculum

Student Books

Grow For It Journal
Grow For It Journal through the Scriptures
What Would Jesus Do? Spiritual Challenge Journal
WWJD Spiritual Challenge Journal: The Next Level
Wild Truth Journal for Junior Highers